THIS WALKER BOOK BELONGS TO:

_____

_____

_____

_____

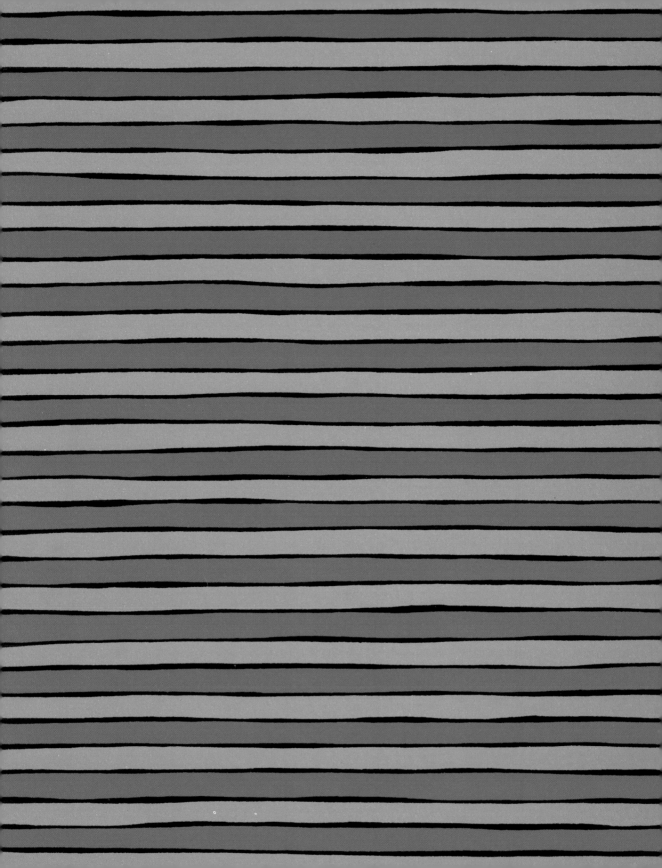

Text first published 1985 by
HarperCollins Publishers Ltd
This edition published 1994
by Walker Books Ltd
87 Vauxhall Walk, London SE11 5HJ

Paperback edition published 1995

This book has been typeset in
Garamond Book Educational.

Printed in Hong Kong

British Library Cataloguing in Publication Data
A catalogue record for this book is available
from the British Library.

ISBN 0-7445-4328-2

Crazy
ABC

Written by
Judy Hindley
Illustrated by
Nick Sharratt

WALKER BOOKS
AND SUBSIDIARIES
LONDON • BOSTON • SYDNEY

Aa

Axe in the apple tree –

what else begins like that?

Ask an alligator

with an apple

on his hat.

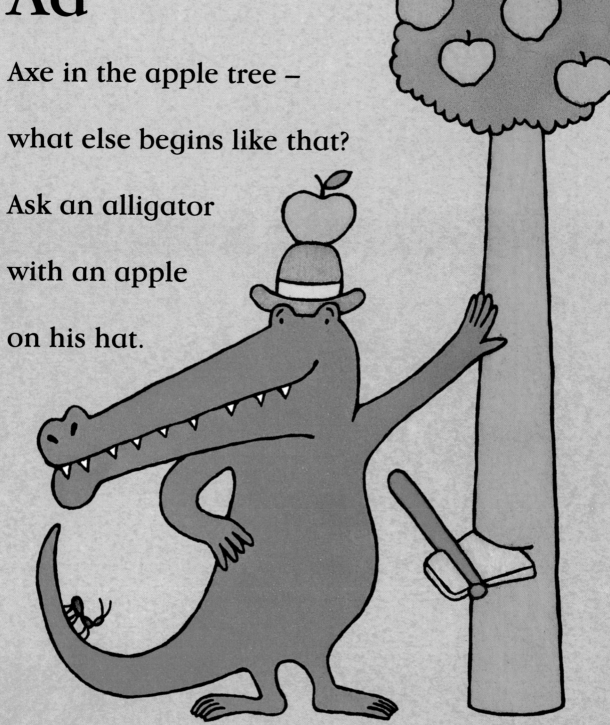

Bb

What can you see

that starts with *b*?

I see three things like that:

a thing that can sing,

a thing that can sting,

and a bat.

Boo, bee! You bother me!

Scat, bat!

Cc

Can you? Can you?

Can you do what I can do?

Can you creep along

like a caterpillar?

Can you curl up

like a cat?

Dd

What do you do

that starts with *d*?

What do you do, my dear?

I dance until I'm dizzy

with a daisy

in my ear.

Ee

'Ello, 'ello, 'ello,

what have we 'ere?

Egg on the edge,

egg on its end,

egg on my elbow –

egg everywhere!

Ff

Fie! Fo!

There's a fly on my nose!

What other funny things

can you see?

A frog on my foot,

a flea on my knee!

Gg

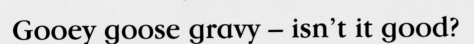

Gooey goose gravy – isn't it good?

Glassful of grape-juice, glug, glug, glug.

Hh

Ho, ho, ho!

How shall I be happy?

I'll hop until I'm happy,

I'll hide until you find me,

and then I'll have a hug.

Ho, ho, ho!

Ii

"Ick!" said the Indian.

"It

is

ITCHY

in

this

outfit!"

Jj

What do you like

that starts with *j*?

Do you like jelly?

Do you like jam?

Do you like to jump

as high as you can?

Kk

Here is a kite

fit for a king!

Here is a king

in the kite string.

Give it a kick!

Ll

Look, look,

look what I can do!

Leap high…

Lie low…

Lick a lovely lolly.

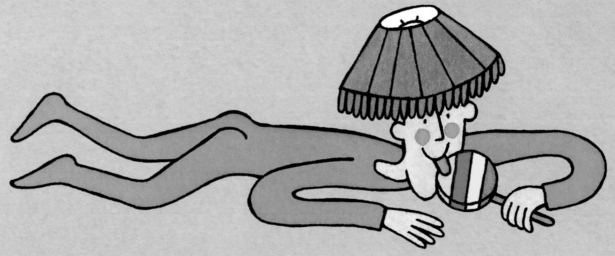

Mm

The mountaineer

has lost his map.

What a mess!

What a muddle!

Oh, where is his mum?

Nn

No, no, no!

This isn't nice!

Here is a ninny

with a nut on his nose,

and a noodle on his necktie!

No, no, no!

Oo

Odd! It's an omelette!

An omelette falling off!

And here we see an officer

with omelette on top.

Pp

"Pooh!" said the pirate,

peering at his plate of prunes.

What a picky peg-leg,

picking at his *p*s.

Can you find the *p*s?

Pickles, pears, potatoes –

look at all of these!

Qq

Queasy, queasy queen.

She must be feeling sick.

Tuck her in a quilt,

quick, quick, quick!

Rr

Rrrm, rrrm, race-track rider,

racing for a ribbon,

ROARS around the race-track,

rrrm, rrrm, rrrm!

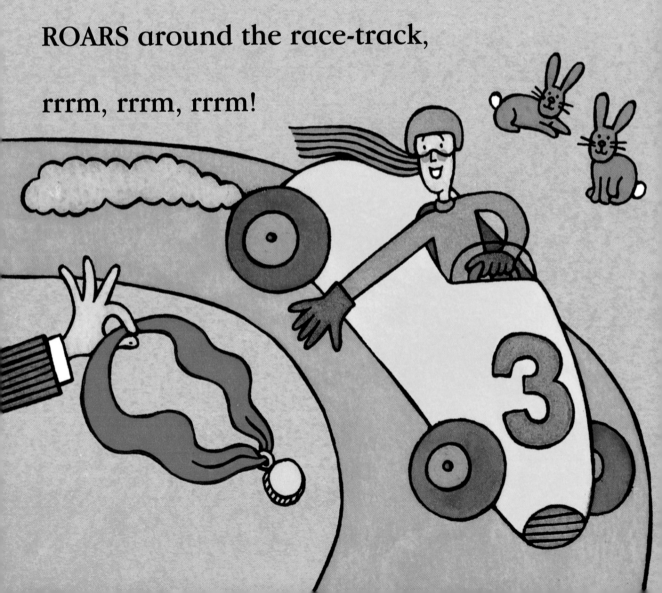

Ss

See here! Sit up straight!

Sip your soup like Mrs Snake.

Sssss – don't slurp!

What a silly sausage!

Tt

Tut, tut, tut,

do you have a *t*?

I have lots of *t*s:

tummy, toes and teeth!

Uu

Up, up, up!

Underneath umbrella.

Upset,

upside down,

making ugly faces.

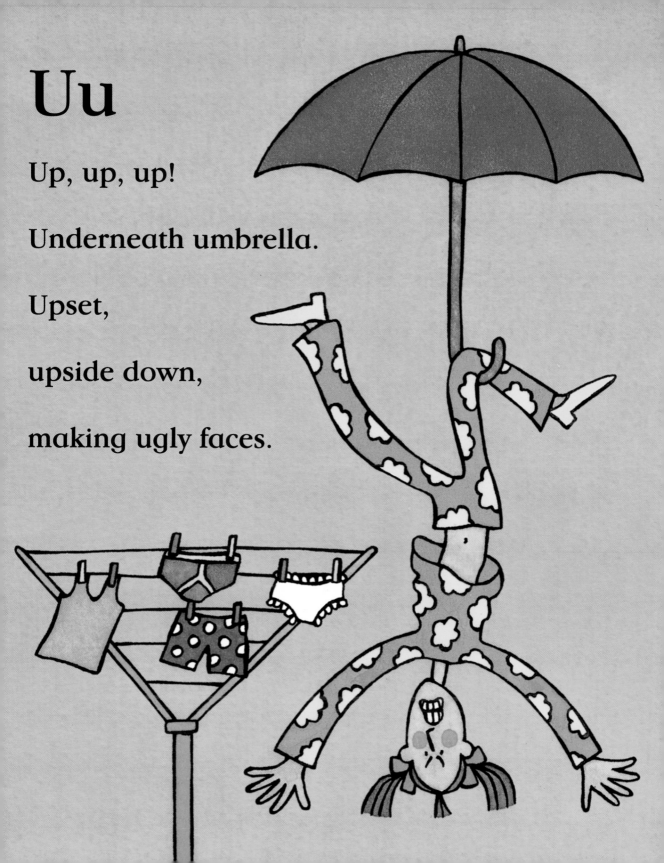

Vv

Vroom! Vroom!

Very fast van!

Very smashed vegetables,

very sad man.

Ww

Woo, woo, wild wind

whistles round your head.

Wiggly worm,

wicked witch,

warm in bed.

Xx

X-ray.

Exit.

Who's next?

Yy

Yippee, yippee! Yellow yacht,

racing round the bend.

Happy, happy yachtsman

when the day is at an end.

Zz

Zipping in,

zipping up.

ZZZZZZZzzzzzz

Good night, my friend.

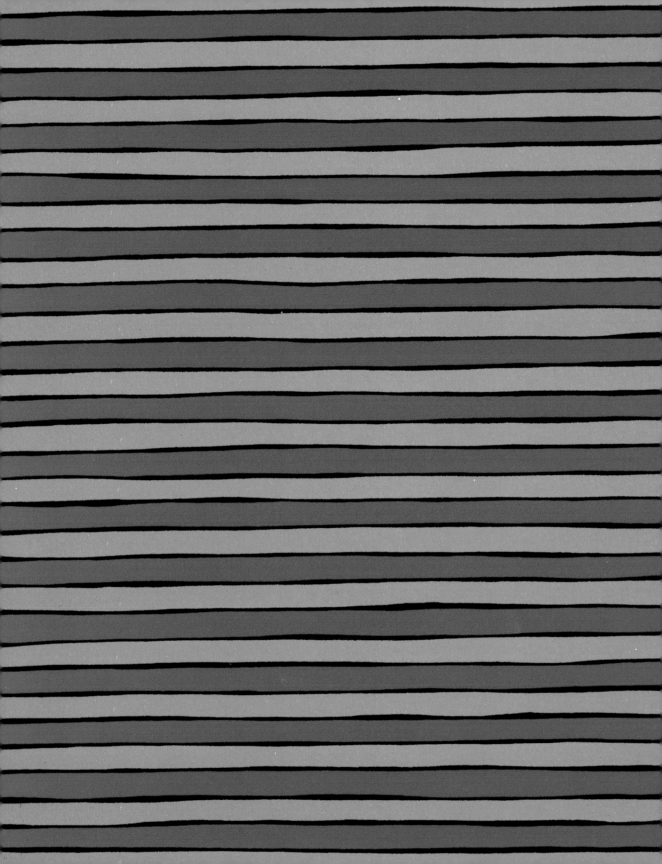

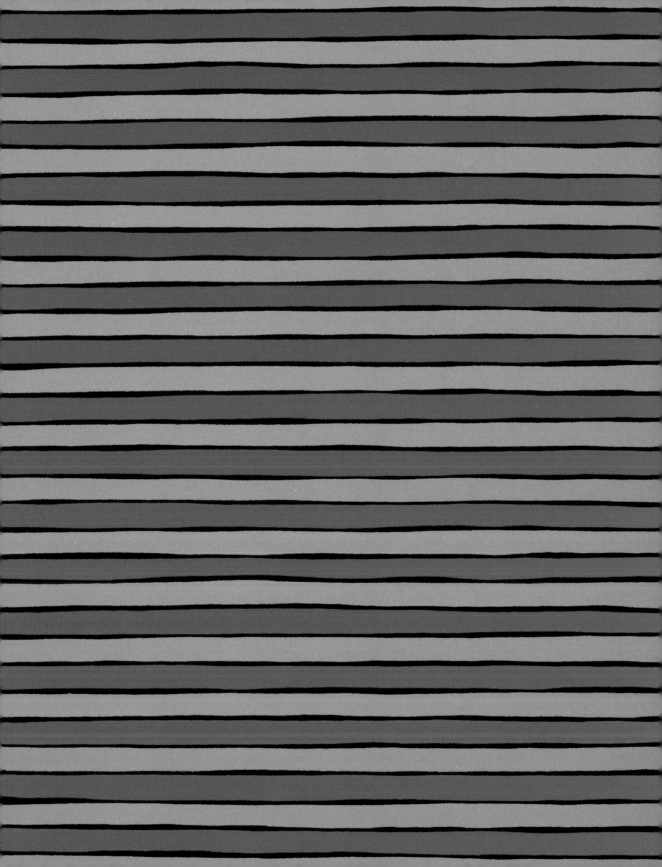

MORE WALKER PAPERBACKS
For You to Enjoy

CRAZY ABC
ISN'T IT TIME?
LITTLE AND BIG
ONE BY ONE
Judy Hindley/Nick Sharratt

There are four books in this series of concept readers –
and they're all equally zany, bright and full of fun!

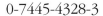

0-7445-4328-3

0-7445-4329-0

0-7445-4330-4

0-7445-4331-2

£3.99 each

INTO THE JUNGLE
Judy Hindley/Melanie Epps

An evocative and playful picture book about two children's
imaginative jungle game. Cries out for readers' participation!

0-7445-2074-6   £3.99

MY MUM AND DAD MAKE ME LAUGH
Nick Sharratt

Mum loves spots, Dad loves stripes but their son has an elephantine
obsession that tops them all!

"Delightful for its brightness and consistency of concept." *The Sunday Times*

0-7445-4307-X   £3.99